Scolosaurus

Written by David White
Illustrated by Pam Mara

Library of Congress Cataloging-in-Publication Data

White, David, 1952 July 13–
  Scolosaurus.

  Summary: Describes the activities, behavior, and physical characteristics of this dinosaur with the spiny tail.
  1. Scolosaurus—Juvenile literature.
[1. Scolosaurus. 2. Dinosaurs] I. Mara, Pamela, ill. II. Title.
QE862.065W454 1988   567.9′7   87-37627
ISBN 0-86592-519-4

Rourke Enterprises, Inc.
Vero Beach, FL 32964

Quetzalcoatlus

Parasaurolphus

Deinosuchus

Corythasaurus

Spinosaurus

Oviraptor

Scolosaurus

Pachycephalosaurus

Anatosaurus

Struthiomimus

Scolosaurus

Rutiodon

Psittacosaurus

The rocks of the foothills cast long shadows in the first sunlight. A python, which had slept against a tree stump during the night, uncurled and slithered away. All was still. Then slowly, one of the rocks began to move. It was Scolosaurus. As he lay flat against the ground the heavy armor on his back made him look like a piece of rugged rock.

Scolosaurus liked the safety of hills. If he could not find a cave or rock for shelter, his camouflage would always protect him. He could also walk more safely there than he could in the swampy forests. There was no danger of getting bogged down.

Now he needed food. The grasses of the mountains were sparse and dry. He wanted the green and juicy plants of the woods. He set off for the trees in the valley below.

Scolosaurus knew a glade where the most succulent foliage grew. Here, magnolia and climbing roses flowered. Bees, attracted by the bright colors, carried pollen from one to the other.

Scolosaurus browsed peacefully among the undergrowth. The peace was soon disturbed by the sound of an animal crashing through the foliage.

Struthiomimus burst into the glade. He was a tall creature, with long legs and a long neck. His three-toed feet enabled him to run away quickly from any attacker. Now he needed to use them.

Close after him came Dromaeosaurus. He was far smaller than Struthiomimus, but much more dangerous. This fierce little animal had wickedly sharp claws on his hind legs, which he used to slash at his victims.

Struthiomimus ran around the glade, dodging this way and that. Speed was his only defense against Dromaeosaurus. Scolosaurus took little notice of the chase. With his heavy armor, he was well protected against creatures like Dromaeosaurus. Only his underbelly was vulnerable to attack. This is why he took so much care to protect it.

After circling the glade, Struthiomimus suddenly darted into the trees. Dromaeosaurus did not bother to follow. The chase had tired him. He turned and retraced his steps. There would be other prey for him.

Now the sun was higher, and the forest grew hotter and more humid. Scolosaurus felt thirsty. It was time for him to go down to the river to drink. The river ran through a plain beyond the wood. As Scolosaurus left the shelter of the trees, he was glad he had the protection of his armor.

Across the river plain, Scolosaurus saw herds of Parasaurolophus and Trachodon. Like him, they were going to the river to drink. Most animals visited the river at some time during the day. This made it a dangerous place. The meat-eaters could be sure of a kill if they lay in wait long enough.

Today, there were no signs of the meat-eaters. Side by side with the Trachodons, Scolosaurus drank the clear water of the river. The only sound to disturb the peace was the buzzing of flying insects and the flutter of dragonflies.

Suddenly, Scolosaurus noticed that the Trachodons beside him had vanished. He could see the reason for this reflected in the river. The image of Gorgosaurus appeared in the water. Scolosaurus twisted around to face him, just as Gorgosaurus lunged forward. The huge jaws and savage teeth of the mighty meat-eater snapped shut close to Scolosaurus's face.

Instinctively, Scolosaurus took up a defensive position. He tucked his great legs under his body and lowered himself to the ground. There was no gap between his armor and the ground. Gorgosaurus circled around him, roaring angrily.

The meat-eater began to lunge at Scolosaurus in an effort to turn him over. This would be the end for Scolosaurus. Quite unprotected and unable to regain his upright position, he would be easy prey for the sharp teeth of Gorgosaurus. He must do everything in his power to prevent it.

Luckily, he was equipped with a heavy tail, and armed with two spikes at the tip. As Gorgosaurus stood astride him, Scolosaurus lashed upward at the meat-eater. Gorgosaurus reeled back, roaring with pain. Gorgosaurus lunged again and the Scolosaurus's tail hit him again just below the throat. Gorgosaurus was almost thrown to the ground.

Finally, Gorgosaurus turned away. He had enough of Scolosaurus and his spiny tail. He moved off down the river bank. This time, it was the Gorgosaurus who was trapped. Facing him was Styracosaurus. With his frill of spikes, he was a fearsome sight. Gorgosaurus hesitated for a moment. If he could get around the side of Styracosaurus, he could deal with him.

Styracosaurus did not give him the chance. With a bellow, he began to charge straight at the meat-eater. The dust flew up behind him as he approached. Gorgosaurus tried to sidestep him, but he was too slow. Styracosaurus landed a stunning blow on his right side.

Gorgosaurus lost his footing and crashed to the ground. Scolosaurus did not wait to see what happened next. Wisely, he took the chance to slip away from the river, across the flood plain toward the woods.

By now it was late afternoon. The shadows had begun to lengthen. The woods looked darker and more threatening. Scolosaurus moved quickly through the undergrowth, as dozens of smaller creatures scampered across his path.

Soon he emerged from the woods, and began the long climb up the foothills to his home. As he climbed, he saw the shape of other animals in the dusk. There was Ankylosaurus, searching for a crevice in the rocks in which to spend the night. Like Scolosaurus, he was safe in the open of the plateaus. He, too, carried heavy armor on his back, and his tail wielded a fearsome club.

Eventually, Scolosaurus reached his resting place. The journey back from the river had been long and he was tired. He sank down, his legs tucked under him. As the sun set and night covered the land, he slept.

Scolosaurus and the Cretaceous World

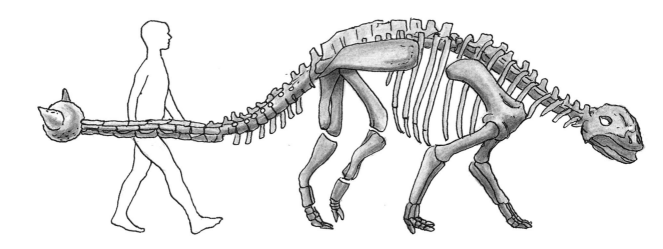

The skeleton of Scolosaurus compared in size with a man

The time of Scolosaurus

Although fossilized remains of Scolosaurus are very rare, there is enough evidence to suggest that Scolosaurus lived at the very end of the age of dinosaurs; that is, in the late Cretaceous period, between 100 million and 65 million years ago. The reason there are so few remains is that Scolosaurus lived in the upland areas, where no sediments were formed. Most of our evidence about dinosaurs comes from sedimentary rocks.

The land of Scolosaurus

The Cretaceous period was a time of immense change. Seas divided the northern supercontinent of Laurasia in two, to form Asiamerica (eastern Asia and western North America) and Euramerica (Europe and eastern North America). The collision of Europe and North and South America, which were joined for the first time, began to push up the present day Rockies and the Andes.

Scientists think that Scolosaurus probably lived at the foot of these new mountain ranges. Scolosaurus must have been a successful dinosaur, since remains have been found throughout the northern hemisphere, in Asia, Europe and North America. No remains have been found in the southern continents of Africa, India, and Australia.

This is because the continents had separated from the northern landmass, so the dinosaurs were no longer able to move from one to the other.

The family tree of Scolosaurus.

Scolosaurus belonged to the family of ankylosaurs, or "armored dinosaurs." The earliest ankylosaur was probably Scelidosaurus, who lived in early Jurassic times, 195 million years ago. The family of more than 30 types of ankylosaurs developed in to two distinct branches. On the one side there were the lightweight ankylosaurs, with narrow heads and without tail weapons. On the other side there were the heavyweight ankylosaurs, armored like tanks and armed with a spike or club on their tails.

Scolosaurs, an advanced member of the ankylosaur family, belonged to the armored branch.

Other plant eaters

Plant-eating dinosaurs dominated the late Cretaceous period. Besides the ankylosaurs, the other main plant-eaters were the hadrosaurs and the ceratopsians. Parasaurolophus, who appears in the story, was a striking-looking hadrosaur, with a hollow crest that measured over six feet from snout to tip. Trachodon, or Anatosaurus as it is alternatively named, was a flat-headed hadrosaur. Both these creatures were harmless and inoffensive creatures. Their defence lay in flight rather than fight.

Other plant-eaters, however, were not so docile. Ceratopsians were like rhinoceroses, with heavy bodies, sturdy legs and horns on their faces. Some of them, like Styracosaurus, had a frill of spikes round their necks. Their formidable features were enough to drive away any meat-eating dinosaur.

Meat-eaters

Carnivorous dinosaurs had an important function in the late Cretaceous period. By preying on the plant-eating dinosaurs, they prevented the forests becoming over-browsed. The most impressive meat-eaters were Tyrannosaurus and his cousin Gorgosaurus, who appears in this story. But other, smaller meat-eaters could be equally fearsome. Dromaeosaurus, one of the family of coelurosaurs, made up for his size with a sickle claw, which he used to attack far larger creatures.

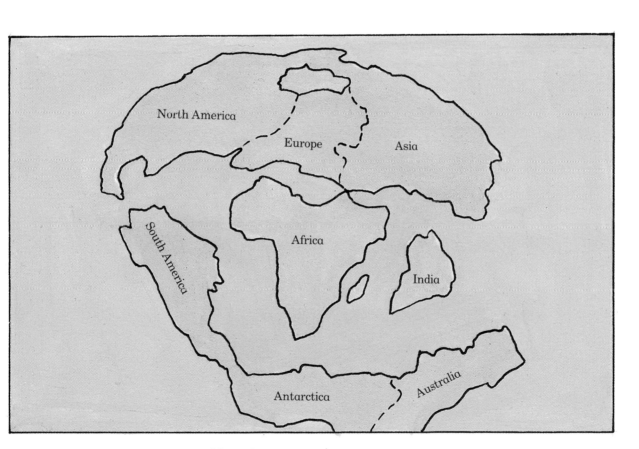

Map of the Cretaceous World